CHINESE FESTIVALS COOKBOOK

STUART THOMPSON AND ANGELA DENNINGTON WITH PHOTOGRAPHY BY ZUL MUKHIDA

RAINTREE
STECK-VAUGHN
PUBLISHERS
RSVP®

A Harcourt Company

Austin   New York
www.steck-vaughn.com

Holiday Cookbooks
from Around the World

Christian Cookbook

Hindu Cookbook

Jewish Cookbook

Chinese Cookbook

Note: Nuts are contained in one of the recipes in this book (see page 28).
Nuts may provoke a dangerous allergic reaction in some people.

Published by Raintree Steck-Vaughn Publishers, an imprint of Steck-Vaughn Company

Library of Congress Cataloging-in-Publication Data
Dennington, Angela and Thompson, Stuart.
Chinese festival cookbook / Stuart Thompson and Angela Dennington.
    p.   cm.—(Holiday cookbooks from around the world)
    Includes bibliographical references and index.
    ISBN 0-7398-3262-X
    1. Chinese cookbook—Juvenile literature.
    [1. Chinese cookbook.]
    I. Title.

Photograph acknowledgments:
Art Directors and TRIP 6, (A. Tovy), 22 (P. Treanor); The Hutchison Library 13, (Liba Taylor), 21 (Christine Pemberton), 29 (Lesley Nelson); Impact Photos 4 (Jonathan Pile), 7 (Simon Shepheard), 23 (Christophe Bluntzer); Wayland Picture Library 6, 14–15 bottom, 15 top (Zul Mukhida).

All instructions, information, and advice given in this book are believed to be reliable and accurate. All guidelines and warnings should be read carefully and the author, packager, editor, and publisher cannot accept responsibility for injuries or damage arising out of failure to comply with the same.

Printed in Italy. Bound in the United States.
1 2 3 4 5 6 7 8 9 0 05 04 03 02 01

Contents

Festivals, Food, and Firecrackers

China is a huge country. Almost a quarter of the world's people live there. Of the hundreds of festivals in the Chinese calendar, some are celebrated throughout China. The most important are the Chinese New Year's festival, the Dragon Boat festival, and the Mid-Autumn festival. Besides these famous occasions, there used to be hundreds of local festivals.

Both famous and local Chinese festivals are occasions for families, friends, or the community to feast and have fun. For children, festivals mean a break from school and for adults a holiday from work. Festivals are times for enjoyment, and one of the things Chinese people like most is good food. Local festivals give families a welcome excuse to invite friends and relatives to holiday banquets.

By sharing a festive meal, Chinese people show friendship, or the feeling that they belong together.

Some festivals are celebrated at a temple with incense, food, and special offerings. This temple is in Hong Kong.

Many Chinese festivals have been celebrated for centuries. At some, families lay out expensive foods. Perfumed smoke from sticks of burning incense respectfully tells gods or ancestors that the food presented is for them. After the gods or ancestors have "tasted" it, the food offerings provide a feast that the people share. At other festivals, families or communities meet to protect themselves from evil or dangerous forces.

SAFETY AND HYGIENE

When cutting with knives, frying, boiling, and using the oven, ALWAYS ask an adult to help you.

Food must always be kept clean. Food that gets dirty will not taste good—and can even make people sick.

Always wash your hands before you start cooking.

Do not wipe dirty hands on a towel. Wash your hands first.

If you need to taste something while cooking, use a clean fork or spoon.

Make sure work surfaces are clean and dry. This includes tables, countertops, and chopping boards.

Chinese festivals are noisy occasions. There's the noise of many people enjoying food, conversation, and gambling or drinking games. At night, crowds gather to watch open-air operas or puppet shows. Noisiest of all are the firecrackers. The Chinese invented gunpowder long ago, but not for fighting battles. Instead, they made fire-crackers to use on special occasions. The ear-piercing sound of exploding fire-crackers tells the world that there is a celebration. The noise is believed to scare away ghosts and harmful creatures.

CHINESE NEW YEAR'S FESTIVAL

Exploding firecrackers welcome in the New Year and encourage the dragon to dance at these celebrations in Guangxi, China.

Chinese festivals are dated according to a lunar (moon) calendar, based on the phases of the moon. The Chinese New Year falls sometime between January 16 and February 21 on the Western solar (sun) calendar. The New Year's Festival marks winter's end and spring's return. So it is also called Spring Festival. Another farming year will soon start, but first there's time for a festive holiday.

Each family prepares many favorite dishes for its New Year's Eve feast. It is a private meal, for family only. Homes are spring-cleaned, debts are paid, new clothing is laid out, and baths are taken, so that everything and everyone is ready for a clean start to the New Year. Roads and trains are packed as family members who live elsewhere return home. It is the most important time for families to be together.

On New Year's Eve the whole family may spend hours making dumplings, or jiaozi (see pages 10–12). Pork is the best-liked meat, but it is good to include chicken (*ji*, pronounced "jee") since it sounds like the word lucky (*ji*); and fish (*yu*, pronounced "you") which sounds like the word riches (*yu*). Cutting up food—or anything else—at New Year's is believed to cause bad luck, though. The festive food should be "whole," like the family.

First, the food is offered to the family's ancestors to show that they are still cared for and remembered. Then, families enjoy the many delicious dishes, staying up late. Next morning, at dawn, screaming blasts of firecrackers noisily announce the New Year. People congratulate their neighbors on surviving to see in another year. It's time to visit friends and relatives. Grandparents give children red packets of "lucky money." The holiday atmosphere lasts two more weeks until the Lantern Festival, after which it's back to work and school.

A man dressed as the "god of money" hands out lucky money envelopes in a festive crowd.

Spring Rolls

Preparation time: 20 minutes

Cooking time: 10 to 20 minutes

Makes: 15 to 20 spring rolls

Ingredients

$1/2$ pound mixed vegetables

5 or 6 ounces ground meat

5 or 6 ounces cooked shrimp

1 tbsp light soy sauce

1 tsp salt

1 package of spring roll wrappers (about 4 inches square), thawed

2 tsp flour, with a little water added to make a paste

$1–1^1/2$ quarts cooking oil

Equipment

Chef's knife

Grater

Wooden spoon

Frying pan (for stir-frying)

Large bowl

Pastry brush

Large deep pan suitable for deep-frying (or electric deep-fryer)

Paper towel

Cookie sheet

Spring rolls, or chunjuan (pronounced "chu-en-juan"), are usually eaten as snacks or as part of a meal. Another name for New Year's is the Spring Festival, since it marks the start of the spring season. *Chun* means "spring," which is why these rolls are a good food to eat at Chinese New Year's.

You can use a variety of vegetables and meat in chunjuan. For vegetables, choose several from cabbage, bean sprouts, bamboo shoots, water chestnuts, mushrooms, leeks, scallions, or carrots. For meat, use pork, beef, chicken, or turkey.

1 With an adult's help, shred or chop the vegetables fine so they are all the same size. Put the ground meat in the bowl. Add the soy sauce and salt.

2 Ask an adult to put a little oil in the frying pan. Heat and stir-fry the meat for 30 seconds. Add the vegetables and stir-fry for another minute.

3 Drain off the juices. Empty the mixture into the bowl. Allow to cool. Chop the shrimp, and mix in well.

4 Lay out a wrapper in a diamond shape. Place two table-spoons of filling near the middle. Fold the bottom flap over the filling, tucking the tip of the pastry under. Roll it over once away from you.

5 Keep one hand on the roll, and fold in each side with your other hand. Brush the remaining triangle flap with flour paste to act as a glue. Roll the filling into a tight cylinder.

6 Ask an adult to heat the oil in a deep-fryer or saucepan. Gently slide in about six rolls. They will float freely. Fry for 4 to 5 minutes, turning them over once.

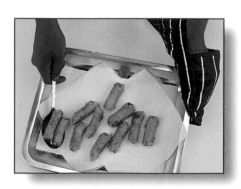

7 When the spring rolls are crisp and golden-brown, lift carefully from the oil with a slotted spoon. Put on the cookie sheet lined with the paper towel. Place in a low oven, leaving door open. Deep-fry the remaining spring rolls.

8 Serve hot and crisp. If you like, flavor with soy sauce, a little vinegar, or maybe ketchup.

Steamed Dumplings

These bite-sized dumplings are known in Chinese as jiaozi (pronounced "gee-ow-dze"). They are often the main Chinese New Year's food. Traditional jiaozi are little pouches of dough filled with ground pork, cabbage, ginger, and scallions, but you can experiment with other savory fillings. Eating dozens of tasty dumplings together is a traditional meal for family gatherings. Everyone, including children, shares in the family teamwork of preparing them.

Preparation time: about 1 hour

Cooking time: 15 minutes per batch of 10 to 12 dumplings

Makes: about 80 dumplings

Ingredients

3³/4 cups all-purpose flour

1 cup cold water

Filling:

4 sticks celery

1¹/2 tsp fresh ginger root (optional)

2 scallions

2 small garlic cloves

¹/2 lb. ground meat (pork, beef, chicken, or turkey)

1 tbsp sesame oil

¹/2 tsp salt

2 tbsp light soy sauce

Dipping sauce:

4 tbsp light soy sauce

4 tbsp vinegar

1 **Wrappers:** mix the flour and water in a bowl and work into a firm, smooth, springy dough. (You may need to add extra flour or water.)

2 Turn the dough on to a lightly floured surface, and knead firmly for about 10 minutes until smooth and elastic. Wrap in plastic wrap while preparing the filling.

Equipment

2 large bowls

Wooden spoons

Chef's knife

Rolling pin

Large saucepan

2 cookie sheets

Slotted spoon

Plastic wrap

3 **Filling:** chop the celery, ginger, green onions, and garlic as fine as possible. Put all the filling ingredients into the mixing bowl. Mix them together well.

4 **Dumpling wrappers:** Divide the dough into four pieces. Keep three pieces under some plastic wrap while you work with the other quarter of the dough.

5 Lightly flour the countertop and keep it floured. Knead the dough lightly once more. Roll into a long sausage about 3/4 inch wide and 12 inches long. Cut into 20 pieces.

6 Flatten a piece of dough with the palm of your hand. Roll from the edge to the center with the rolling pin. Then turn it 90 degrees and roll again. Keep going until you have a circle of about 3 inches across, thinner at the edge and thicker in the middle.

7 **Filling dumplings:** Lay out 10 to 12 dumpling wrappers. Place a heaping teaspoon of the filling in the center of each circle, keeping clear of the edges.

8 Carefully lift a wrapper and filling. Cradle it between your thumb and first finger. With your other hand, pinch the sides of the wrapper together firmly to make a well-sealed fan-shaped purse.

Steamed Dumplings (continued)

9 Put the dumplings separately on a floured cookie sheet, ready for cooking. Keep making dumplings until the wrappers and filling are used up. Mix the dipping sauce.

10 Cooking dumplings: Fill the saucepan half full of water. Ask an adult to bring it to a boil. Using a slotted spoon, put in 10 to 12 dumplings, one by one, and stir gently, being careful not to puncture the wrappers.

11 Bring the water back to a gentle boil. Boil for 2 minutes. Remove from the heat for 10 minutes. Then bring back to a gentle boil once more. Lift the dumplings out with a slotted spoon. Repeat steps 10 and 11 with the rest of the dumplings.

12 Serve with a separate bowl of dipping sauce. Eat immediately. Repeat until all the dumplings have been cooked— and eaten.

THE SURVIVAL OF NEW YEAR

Some years ago, the Chinese government strongly disapproved of traditional festivals and tried to stop people from celebrating them. They regarded festivals as a waste of time, money, and effort. They saw festivals as based on superstitious ideas, and as a way for the rich to cheat the poor.

So the government banned many festivals, or forced people to have simpler and less costly festivals. Instead they created new ones, like Workers' Day (May 1), Children's Day (June 1), National Day (October 1), and Women's Day (March 8).

But most people did not like these changes. They felt the new holidays were boring: no crowds, no color, no gambling, no noisy firecrackers—and not even the opportunity to enjoy delicious festive food with family and friends, because the government criticized banquets as wasteful.

The Chinese New Year is celebrated in many different countries where Chinese people live. This food stand in London's Soho serves large spring rolls and other snacks for everyone to enjoy.

Now the government does not interfere as much when people want to celebrate traditional festivals. So once more in China, as for many Chinese people around the world, the traditional Chinese New Year is the most important festival for the family to celebrate, usually by enjoying a magnificent meal together.

Dragon Boat Festival

For hundreds of years there have been dragon boat races on the fifth day of the fifth (lunar) month. It is an ancient sports festival held when the summer sun is at its highest in the sky. Another name for the festival is Poet's Day. At school, Chinese children learn the story of why dragon boats are raced on Poet's Day.

The poet Qu Yuan (pronounced "Chu Yu-an") lived more than 2,000 years ago. He was also an important politician and was very honest and patriotic. He believed that it was his duty to do everything he could for his country, China. When the corrupt ruler refused to listen to his advice, Qu Yuan felt he had to make the strongest possible complaint. So, in protest, he threw himself into a lake to drown. When local fishermen realized he was drowning, they raced their boats at full speed to save him. They beat drums to frighten off fish, which they feared might eat him. They threw bags of rice into the water for the fish to feed on instead. But they were too late. The poet's body was never found.

The Dragon Boat Festival is held in Qu Yuan's honor. The boats have a dragon's head carved at the front. Crews race to the beat of their boat's drum.

Zongzi, packets of leaf-wrapped rice, are the festival's most famous food. They are given as gifts during the fifth month. Barbecue roast pork is a welcome dish at any time, but it tastes best to winning crews! In the summer heat, though, mung bean soup is a good "cooling" food.

Farmers need summer rain for a good harvest. Perhaps dragon-boat racing encourages rain, since, in Chinese tradition, heavy rain is said to result from dragons fighting in the sky.

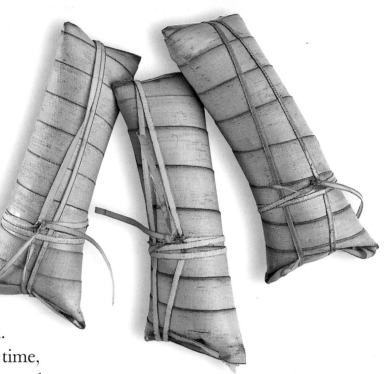

Zongzi are often given as gifts during the fifth month.

A traditional dragon boat and crew in southern China. The drum that is beaten for the rowers to follow is the round shape near the front of the boat.

Sticky Rice

Preparation time: 1 hour

Cooking time: 1 hour

Makes: about 10 zongzi

Ingredients

1 cup short-grain, or "sushi" rice

4 slices cooked bacon, plus

2 hard-boiled eggs, all chopped and mixed together

Soy sauce

Equipment

Large saucepan

Wooden spoon

Large bowl

Medium bowl

10 pieces of foil, about 8 inches square

20 pieces of string, about 12 inches long

Steamer

These rice packets, which are usually wrapped in bamboo or lotus leaves, are easily the most famous food for the Dragon Boat Festival. Zongzi (pronounced "dzong-dze") are usually pyramid shaped, but they can be other shapes. The bamboo-leaf wrapping gives a special flavor to the rice. The stuffing inside can be sweet or savory.

Since it is hard to find bamboo leaves, this recipe has been adapted to use aluminum foil to make the packets.

1 Put the rice in a saucepan. Rinse several times. Drain. Add 1 cup of water. With an adult's help, bring it to a boil, stirring often. Simmer until the water is almost all absorbed.

2 Turn the heat very low. Cover with lid. Cook for another 20 minutes. Spoon the rice into a large bowl, and allow to cool.

3 Lay out a piece of foil. Add 3 or 4 tablespoons of cooked rice, with some of the bacon-and-egg filling in the center.

4 Wrap up the foil, folding in the edges until the rice is completely enclosed.

5 Secure by firmly tying with one piece of string. Use a second piece of string to criss-cross the first.

6 Put 1 quart of water in the saucepan. Put the packets into the steamer. Ask an adult to bring the water to a boil, then turn the heat down to a simmer. Place the steamer over the hot water and steam the packets for 1 hour.

7 Carefully unwrap each packet and serve hot. You can flavor the rice with some soy sauce.

Charsiu Roast Pork

Preparation time: 1 hour

Cooking time: 1¹/₂ hours

Oven temperature:
400°F

Ingredients

About 2¹/₂ lb lean pork with a little fat on it, from a pork roast or a pork tenderloin

2 tbsp hoisin sauce

4 tbsp light soy sauce

4 tbsp sugar

1 teaspoon salt

2 tbsps honey

Equipment

Chef's knife

Large bowl

Spoons

Plastic wrap

Wire rack (for roasting)

Roasting pan

Small saucepan

Pastry brush

This is a well-known dish from Canton, in southern China. It is often displayed in Cantonese restaurants, hanging from hooks in the window. It can be eaten cold, so it is convenient for picnics. Sliced up small, charsiu pork (pronounced "char-see-oo") is an ingredient in stir-fried or noodle dishes. Children tend to like it best inside steamed buns.

1 Ask an adult to cut the meat into long strips about 1¹/₂" wide and ³/₄" thick. Score along the strip with diagonal cuts every 2 inches or so.

2 Put the hoisin sauce, soy sauce, sugar, and salt into a bowl. Mix well. Add the meat pieces. Turn them over to cover them evenly in the marinade.

3 Cover the bowl with plastic wrap. Let stand for 2 to 3 hours, turning the meat over twice to spread the marinade evenly.

4 Ask an adult to preheat the oven. Put the meat pieces on the wire rack with the roasting pan underneath. Add water to the roasting pan until it is about ³/₄-inch deep. (It should not touch the meat.)

5 Roast for about 30 minutes. Then take meat pieces out and dip again in the marinade. Replace them upside down on the rack. Roast for another 20 to 30 minutes.

6 Reduce the oven heat if the sauce starts to burn. Check that the meat is cooked by sticking a knife into it. If the juice is clear, the meat is cooked. Remove from the oven.

7 Meanwhile, bring the leftover marinade to a boil with the honey, and simmer for about 20 minutes. Brush evenly over the roasted meat while hot.

8 Cut the roasted meat into slices, about ¹/₄-inch thick. Serve hot or cold.

Mung Bean Soup

Preparation time: Overnight

Cooking time: 2¹/₄ hours

Serves: 6

Ingredients

¹/₂ lb green mung beans

1¹/₂ quarts water

³/₄ cup sugar

Equipment

Large bowl

Large saucepan

This sweet green soup is known as Ludou Tang (pronounced "loo-doe tang"), and is popular in southern China. People think that drinking it has a "cooling" effect in the hot summer.

Chinese people do not usually have a dessert after their meal. Instead they may round off their meal with fresh fruit and Chinese tea. There is a wide variety of cakes, snacks, and sweet soups to eat between meals or in the late evening.

1 Rinse the mung beans thoroughly several times.

2 In a large bowl, leave the beans to soak overnight in 1 quart of cold water. Do not drain.

3 Transfer the beans and water to a large saucepan. Add another 2 cups of cold water.

4 With an adult's help, bring to a boil. Then reduce the heat, cover, and simmer for 2 hours. Stir occasionally.

5 Add the sugar. Simmer until the sugar has completely dissolved.

6 Serve hot. But it can be eaten cold, or frozen into popsicles!

OTHER DRAGON BOAT CELEBRATIONS

Though the Dragon Boat Festival was banned for some years in China, the boat races have now become a worldwide activity.

Every year since 1976, World Championship International Dragon Boat Races have been held in Hong Kong harbor, with over 100 teams from more than 20 countries taking part. There are Dragon Boat clubs and competitions not only in China, Hong Kong, Taiwan, and Singapore, but also in the United States, Canada, Holland, Germany, Great Britain, and Australia.

The dragon boat races held in Hong Kong are a colorful sight, and many people flock to watch them.

On the whole, Dragon Boat Racing has become a popular sport, and, because it is unusual and quite spectacular to watch, the competitions are often held to raise money for charities.

Although zongzi are very popular for this festival, not many people outside China make their own, partly because it is not easy to find the bamboo or lotus leaves for the wrapping. However, many Chinese supermarkets sell uncooked zongzi in May or June, around the time of the festival.

21

MiD-AUTUMN FESTiVAL

Chinese New Year's occurs when the spring sun starts to reappear. At the Dragon Boat Festival, the summer sun is at its highest point. At the Mid-Autumn Festival, the sun is weakening. People focus, instead, on the full moon, which is said to be the year's brightest and roundest.

This is a time for families to get together, and for the living to remember their ancestors. Families gather together to "admire the moon," so this festival is also called the Moon Festival. People eat evening meals outdoors.

Traditionally, by this time, farmers have gathered in their harvest, storing it for the winter ahead. So the Mid-Autumn Festival is also a harvest festival. Many fruits, especially those that are round like the moon, such as melons, are sold in night markets.

During the Mid-Autumn Festival, many people enjoy evening picnics outdoors, by the light of colorful lanterns, in parks or on hillsides.

Much of the food enjoyed at this festival is round-shaped, to remind people of the moon. These women are making rice balls similar to those on page 28.

The Moon Festival is supposed to be mostly for women to enjoy, since the moon is said to be female. A famous legend tells how a beautiful princess stole and swallowed pills, which gave her immortality. As a punishment she was turned into a toad, and banished to the moon. Look carefully at the full moon to see if you can spot her shadow.

The festival also marks how, 600 years ago, Chinese people rebelled successfully against Mongolian rulers. Important messages about how and when to rebel were secretly distributed to households by hiding them in moon cakes (see pages 24 to 25).

Moon Cakes

Moon cakes, or yuebing (pronounced "you-eh-bing"), are the main holiday food. They are rich in ingredients and costly to buy. One traditional filling has salted duck egg yolk in a sweet, dark, lotus-seed purée. Slicing through the moon cake is said to reveal "the golden moon in a dark sky." This recipe is adapted here, using puréed figs instead of lotus-seed purée, and a dried apricot for the salted duck egg.

Preparation: 1 1/2 hours

Cooking time: 30 minutes

Oven temperature: 400°F

Makes: 20

Ingredients

3 3/4 cups self-rising flour

3 tbsp vegetable oil

3 eggs

1/2 cup sugar

3 tbsp water

1 lb "ready to eat" dried figs

20 "ready to eat" dried apricots

1 egg yolk

Equipment

Food processor (optional), OR
    Large mixing bowl and
    Wooden spoon

Chef's knife

Cookie sheet

Fork

Small bowl

Pastry brush

1 Mix the flour, oil, eggs, sugar, and water together. (Do this in a bowl, by hand, or ask an adult to use a food processor.) Let the pastry rest in the refrigerator for 30 minutes.

2 With an adult's help, cut the figs into small pieces, then mash into a purée. This is easiest in a food processor.

3 Wrap each apricot in fig purée, to make a small ball with the apricot in the center.

4 Divide the pastry into four pieces, then each piece into 5, to make 20 equal portions. Using the palm of your hand, flatten each pastry portion into a 4-inch circle.

5 Wrap each pastry circle around a ball of fig purée (with an apricot inside it). Press the edges of the pastry together tightly to seal the muffin-shaped cake. Ask an adult to preheat the oven.

6 Turn each cake over so the sealed side is on the bottom. Put on an oiled cookie sheet. The finished cakes should be 2½ to 3 inches in diameter, and about ¾ inch high. Prick each cake with a fork.

7 Beat the egg yolk, and then brush it lightly onto each cake. Bake in the oven for 30 minutes, or until golden brown.

Red Hard-boiled Eggs

Red-dyed boiled eggs, or hongshao dan (pronounced "hong-shou dan"), are an appropriate Moon Festival food, since they are round, and red, the Chinese color for happy events. "Red-cooking" is a famous type of Chinese cooking in which food is simmered slowly and for a long time in soy sauce. The soy sauce colors the food a dark brownish-red.

Cooking time: 45 minutes

Serves: 6 to 8

Ingredients

4 to 6 eggs

2/3 cup soy sauce

3/4-inch piece fresh ginger, peeled and bruised

1 tsp Chinese five-spice powder or mixed cinnamon and ground cloves

1 tbsp sugar

1/2 tsp salt

1/2 cup water

Equipment

Small saucepan

1 Ask an adult to help you boil the eggs for 5 minutes. When cooked, rinse the eggs under cold running water to cool them down.

2 When the eggs are cool, remove their shells.

3 Put the soy sauce, ginger, five-spice powder, sugar, salt, and water in the saucepan, and bring to a simmer. Continue to simmer for 2 minutes to allow the ginger flavor to get into the sauce.

4 With an adult's help, place the peeled eggs carefully into the simmering sauce. Turn each egg so the sauce coats it evenly.

5 Let the eggs cook in the sauce for about half an hour. Turn them over occasionally to get an even coating of the sauce.

6 Serve the eggs with the red-cooked sauce. It tastes very good placed on a bed of plain boiled rice. To eat them cold, let the eggs cool in the sauce. Lift them out to eat whole—with your fingers—or slice them and put them in sandwiches.

Sweet Rice Balls

Preparation time: 1 hour

Cooking time: 10 minutes

Makes: 24 balls

Ingredients

¹/₄ cup fine-ground nuts

2 tbsp butter or margarine

4 tbsp sugar

1¹/₃ cups glutinous rice flour

Water

Equipment

Small mixing bowl

Tablespoon

Large mixing bowl

Knife

Large saucepan

These sweet rice-flour balls, or tangyuan (pronounced "tang-yu-en"), "stick together as families should," and are a "warming" food for the coming winter. They can come in two colors: red or white. They do not always have fillings. In this recipe, a selection of fine-ground nuts—hazel, almond, or walnut— is used. You can select the nuts according to your taste.

1 Mix together the ground nuts, butter, and 2 tablespoons of sugar. Let the mixture chill in the refrigerator for 30 minutes.

2 Make a dough by mixing the glutinous rice flour with enough water to make a smooth, fairly dry dough. Knead it until it is smooth and springy.

3 Roll into a long sausage shape, about 1 inch in diameter and 12 inches long. Cut into 24 pieces. Roll each piece into a ball.

4 Divide the nut mixture into 24 pieces, and roll each piece into a little ball.

5 Use your thumb to make a deep dent in each ball of dough. Insert a little ball of filling into this dent. Close the dough to cover the filling, and roll into a smooth ball again. Do this for all 24 rice balls.

6 In a saucepan, put the remaining 2 tablespoons of sugar in 1 quart of water. With an adult's help, bring it to a boil. Put the rice balls in gently. Cook at medium heat for 5 minutes, or until the balls rise to the surface. Serve hot with the liquid they are cooked in.

OTHER MID-AUTUMN CELEBRATIONS

For about 15 years, until the 1980s, stores in China stopped selling moon cakes. That was because the Chinese government did not like the celebration of the old festivals. Now there are a huge number of different moon cakes available in the autumn in all of China's towns and cities. In countries outside China where many Chinese people have settled, moon cakes are becoming quite a common sight in September or October. In China, the original moon cakes were probably not sweet. They could contain bits of fatty meat as well as other ingredients. Nowadays, in China and elsewhere, most moon cakes are sweet, though many include a duck's or hen's egg yolk.

In the West, moon cakes are often brought in from Hong Kong or Taiwan and sold in attractive tins. They are not cheap—unless you make them yourself!

Except in places where the people are Chinese—such as Hong Kong, Singapore, and Taiwan—the Moon Festival is not celebrated so much. Sometimes, though, a Chinese language school or community group will hold a party using the Mid-Autumn Festival as a focus for a celebration. For both Chinese and non-Chinese people, these days make a convenient excuse to eat lots of good Chinese dishes.

Moon cakes on sale in Hong Kong, with their decorated tins stacked above

↑
year 1972

Besides jiaozi (dumplings) at New Year's meals, there is usually a whole fish dish, and round-shaped foods (such as whole eggs or sweet rice balls). The meaning is that families will be "complete" and "together" in the year to come.

> When using the recipes contained in this book, children should be supervised by one or more adults at all times. This especially applies when cutting with knives, cooking on the stove-top, and using the oven.

Often there is a sticky New Year's cake. The word for cake sounds like the word for "tall" or "high," so eating cake is a way of hoping for success. Some families enjoy a sticky-rice pudding decorated with various dried fruits, called *babaofan*: "eight jewels rice."

Another major Chinese festival, which occurs in early April, is called the Clear and Bright (*Qingming*) Festival. Families go to the tombs of their ancestors to show them that they have not been forgotten. They may bring baskets of food and burn spirit money and incense for the ancestors. Some families have a special picnic meal at the graveside. Others return home to share a family banquet as their way of remembering those members of their family who are no longer alive.

EQUIPMENT
The traditional pan for cooking Chinese food is a wok, which is curved like a large bowl. Using a wok with children is not always a good idea, since woks are easy to tip over during cooking. A thick-bottomed frying pan will be safer and easier to use.

COOKING METHODS
Jiaozi (dumplings) do not be put off by the length of this recipe. This delicious food is surprisingly easy to make and worth the effort. To make the wrappers easy to handle, keep them well dusted with flour. To seal them successfully, it may help to dip your finger in water and run it around the edge of each wrapper before pinching it together.

Vegetarian dumplings can be made with a vegetable filling such as cabbage and carrots. See Chunjuan (spring rolls).

Zongzi these rice packets are traditionally wrapped in bamboo leaves. Dried bamboo leaves can be bought in Chinese supermarkets. To use them, soak first in boiling water for 5 minutes, then drain and cool before wrapping around the filling.

The recipe here gives a savory filling, but a sweet filling can be used instead: insert a spoonful of canned sweetened chestnut or lotus-seed purée.

INGREDIENTS
Note: Please be aware that nuts are contained in the Sweet Rice Balls (page 28). Nuts may provoke an allergic reaction in some people.

Spring roll wrappers Thin squares, available in some Asian supermarkets. It is possible to use Greek filo pastry instead, but it is more brittle and tends to spit during deep-frying.

Glutinous rice This is a traditional Chinese rice that sticks together when it is cooked.

Glutinous rice flour Made from ground glutinous rice.

Mung beans Small, round, green beans, commonly used in the West for sprouting.

GLOSSARY

Ancestors Grandparents, great-grandparents, great-great-grandparents, and so on; the line of family that a person is descended from.

Banned Not allowed, forbidden.

Banquet A special dinner or feast, for many people.

Centuries Hundreds of years.

Congratulate To tell someone "well done!"

Corrupt Cheating, evil.

Debts What you owe; money you should pay back.

Dragon A legendary animal that breathes fire. It is said that Chinese dragons are powerful creatures that can help human beings.

Immortality Being able to live forever and never die.

Incense A powder that gives off a sweet smell when burned.

Gambling Risking money in the hope of winning more money. If you don't win, then you lose your money.

Government The group of people that rules or leads a country.

Local Belonging to a small area or particular place.

Lunar To do with the moon.

Lunar calendar The Chinese calendar based on the phases of the moon. New moon is the first of the month, and full moon is always on the 15th of the month. There are 29 days in a month. To agree with the Western calendar, in some years there is a 13th month.

Patriotic Loving and caring for one's country.

Politician A person who is part of the government.

Rebelled Protested against the government; refused to obey orders.

Savory Salty and spiced, not sweet-tasting.

Solar To do with the sun.

Superstitious Having faith in luck and magic.

Western Belonging to Europe, the United States, Canada, Australia, or New Zealand.

INDEX

Page numbers in **bold** refer to photographs.

RESOURCES

Beatty, Theresa M. *Food and the Recipes of China.* Powerkids Press, 1999.

Burckhardt, Ann L. *The People of China and Their Food.* Capstone Press, 1996.

Russell, Ching Yeung. *Moon Festival.* Boyds Mills Press, 1997.

Shui, Amy, and Stuart Thompson. *China* (Food and Festivals series). Raintree Steck-Vaughn, 1999.